Multiple-Cat Households

Carolyn M. Vella and John J. McGonagle, Jr.

Photographers: Carrie Albert, Joan Balzarini, Richard K. Blackmon, Isabelle Francais, Gillian Lisle, John J. McGonagle, Robert Pearcy, Vince Serbin, John Tyson, Carolyn M. Vella

© T.F.H. Publications, Inc.

Distributed in the UNITED STATES to the Pet Trade by T.F.H. Publications, Inc., 1 TFH Plaza, Neptune City, NJ 07753; on the Internet at www.tfh.com; in CANADA by Rolf C. Hagen Inc., 3225 Sartelon St., Montreal, Quebec H4R 1E8; Pet Trade by H & L Pet Supplies Inc., 27 Kingston Crescent, Kitchener, Ontario N2B 2T6; in ENGLAND by T.F.H. Publications, PO Box 74, Havant PO9 5TT; in AUSTRALIA AND THE SOUTH PACIFIC by T.F.H. (Australia), Pty. Ltd., Box 149, Brookvale 2100 N.S.W., Australia; in NEW ZEALAND by Brooklands Aquarium Ltd., 5 McGiven Drive, New Plymouth, RD1 New Zealand; in SOUTH AFRICA by Rolf C. Hagen S.A. (PTY.) LTD., P.O. Box 201199, Durban North 4016, South Africa; in JAPAN by T.F.H. Publications. Published by T.F.H. Publications, Inc.
MANUFACTURED IN THE
UNITED STATES OF AMERICA
BY T.F.H. PUBLICATIONS, INC.

CONTENTS

3 9082 08741 2154

More than half of all cat-owning households in the United States have more than one cat. Clearly, two heads (and tails) are more fun than one!

INTRODUCTION

Are there a lot of multiple-cat households? Yes. According to the American Veterinary Medical Association (AVMA), the multiple-cat household is becoming increasingly common in the US. Consider the following: The total number of cats owned by Americans continues to increase, and this growth is due *exclusively* to the fact that the number of cats per household has been increasing. In the latest year for which the AVMA has data, a majority of all US households with cats had two or more cats, and the fastest growing group of cat owners was the household with four or more cats.

Why has this occurred? Cats have long been America's most popular household pet, and changes in lifestyle often turn the single-cat household into the multiple-cat household. Increasingly, people feel more comfortable with the idea of taking care of several cats after having experienced the joy of owning one.

Sometimes, too, people may find themselves forced to become a multiple-cat household. Take for example, a few typical situations:

• A family is "adopted" by a stray mother cat and her litter of kittens. Unable to find homes for all of the cats, the family keeps several of them.

• An adult child is newly divorced. She temporarily moves back in with her parents, bringing her two cats with her to join the household's current single feline resident.

• A single adult is taken seriously ill. A nearby friend agrees to take care of the house and its four resident cats. However, the friend has no experience with cat care, much less with the special issues of multiple-cat care.

• A parent dies, leaving a small estate and two older cats to a child. The surviving child is directed to take care of these senior felines, in a household that has two kittens already.

Regardless of how you become a multiple-cat household, as a member of one you face all of the same issues that the owner of a single cat faces—and many others as well. We will try to help those who live in, or may soon live in, a multiple-cat household to understand the special issues that they will face. Of course, every responsible cat owner should already have spent time learning what is involved with basic cat care, such as proper feeding, proper veterinary care, and proper housing. We will touch on these basic matters while discussing the unique issues of the multiple-cat household.

If a stray mother cat and her kittens show up on a family's doorstep, odds are that the family will soon be a multiple-cat household.

Each cat you own will be happy and well loved if you arm yourself with the right information about basic cat care.

WHAT CAN YOU HANDLE?

How many cats *can* you handle? Probably not as many as you think. There are several factors that limit your ability to care for cats. Consider these questions:

• How old are you, and how old are your cats? Remember that as you get older, so do your cats. Older cats, like older people, will tend to need more care, more attention from you, and more medical attention.

• Are you in good health? Caring for cats requires physical work. You have to feed them, which involves carrying bags and cans of cat food, not to mention those heavy bags of litter. You have to be able to move furniture to find a shy new member of the household. You have to be strong enough to capture, restrain, and cage a cat that is ill or hurt and needs attention.

• Do you have enough money? Cats need food, litter, and attention every day. They need yearly veterinary exams and inoculations. Individual cats will need spaying or neutering and routine teeth cleaning. None of these costs will go down, they will only go up, and there are still other financial issues to consider. For example, you should have enough carriers on hand so that in case of emergency, you can put all of your cats in carriers and evacuate them at once. That is just one special expense you must plan for in the multiple-cat household.

• Do you have the time? What does your job require of you? Do you travel a great deal? If so, that could mean

While people of all ages benefit from the joys of pet ownership, potential multiple-cat owners should take their own age and health status into consideration before acquiring new pets.

Just how many cats can you handle? There are many different questions to consider before you become a multiple-cat owner. The authors, breeders of the Japanese Bobtail cats pictured here and throughout, own more than a dozen well-cared-for kitties.

you need to pay a cat-sitter to come in every day. Do you work unusual hours? Many pet supply stores will not be open when you have the time to shop there. When you get home, will you always have the time and physical energy to perform the daily work that caring for a multiple-cat household entails?

• Do you have available sources of help? What would happen if you fell and broke your arm, so that you were in a cast for a month? Is there anyone who can help out?

• How much space do you have? While each cat does not take up a lot of space, you want to make sure that all of your cats have enough room.

Some cats in your household will always be in close proximity to each other, while others prefer to maintain a comfortable distance.

Cats that feel too crowded may react by becoming more aggressive. Also, you may need to separate cats temporarily or permanently for many reasons—health, fear, aggression, medical treatment, etc. Do you have rooms that they can use without coming into contact with the rest of the cats? Do you have plenty of secure space to store cat food and litter, especially if you are in an area where winter travel may become difficult?

For the sake of your cats, and for your own sake, you should underestimate the number of cats you can care for. The limit on how many you can care for is not set by your feelings but by many other factors. By being responsible at the beginning, you can give each of the cats in your household the love, attention, and special care she deserves. Besides, you will still have time, space, and money to yourself. The goal is to enjoy your feline friends and never view them as a burden.

HOW MANY CATS CAN HANDLE EACH OTHER?

It can be difficult to estimate how many cats can live comfortably together. Sometimes you cannot tell which cats will tolerate each other until they are together. There are a few things you should keep in mind as you consider adding a new member to your feline household.

Some cats can be very clannish. You can spot these cats as part of a group that always seems to be together, whether playing, sleeping, or

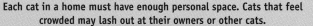

Each cat in a home must have enough personal space. Cats that feel crowded may lash out at their owners or other cats.

Many cats are loners, and these cats can be unhappy in a multiple-cat household. Be sensitive to your beloved pet's feelings—she may need to be your only pet.

eating. If all of your cats are a part of the same group, it may be difficult for a newcomer to fit in. On the other hand, if you have several groups, a newcomer has a better chance of finding new friends in one group if she is not accepted easily by another.

Some cats are loners. They prefer your company to that of other cats, or no company at all. If they feel too crowded, they may react in any number of ways. For example, they might become aggressive towards the newcomer, always move out of the room when the newcomer enters, or they may make litter box "mistakes."

All cats need places where they can get away from even the best of feline friends. So you need to make sure there is more vacant "cat space" for a newcomer.

It is usually much easier for a younger cat or kitten to join a group than it is for an older cat. A younger cat or kitten will find a friend more quickly than an older cat that is more set in her ways.

Most cat households are organized in a hierarchy, just

No matter how social they are, all cats need to be by themselves sometimes.

as lions are in the wild. That is, at the top of the cat pyramid is an older cat—often a male, but sometimes a female that had kittens before she was spayed. The top cat may feel challenged if a cat of about his or her own age and of the same sex comes into the household, even if the new cat does not try to fill that top role. This can make it hard for the newcomer to be accepted, since the top cat will take every opportunity to show her who's boss. It is a very natural reaction, which is based in the wild on a series of complex factors including feeding and reproduction. This is also true for the domestic cats in your household, even though they do not hunt for food and have all been spayed or neutered.

Capitation laws in some locales place a limit of ten on the number of pets allowed in one household. In such a community, this household would have one too many.

LEGAL ISSUES

While it sounds strange, there can be some legal issues involved if you have a large number of cats. There are two major issues to be concerned about. The first, of course, is the general laws providing for the protection of cats, i.e., the humane laws. The second issue is capitation laws.

Problems with the humane laws probably sound farfetched to you. While you are going to take very good care of your cats and kittens, you must be aware of the fact that there are some people who are not as caring as you are. For that reason, it is possible that the local animal welfare officer might visit your home and ask to look around. He might be there because a neighbor or passerby is concerned about your ability to care for so many cats, or he might be following up on a report of a stray cat that has hurt someone. There are a variety of reasons for such a call.

If animal welfare personnel stop by, you can legally refuse to let them in. However, if they have a warrant, that is, a court order, they can come in even if you do not want them to. Why would they get a warrant? Frankly, it would be because they are concerned that the conditions in which your cats are kept are inhumane.

If animal welfare personnel stop by for any reason, your house doesn't need to be spotless. However, your cats must never show signs of neglect.

Your cats should be kept inside. Outdoor cats are subjected to all kinds of danger, from cars to predators.

Now, don't worry. If you have not cleaned the house that day, that doesn't qualify as inhumane treatment, but it does mean that you must take good care of your cats all of the time. That applies even when you are not home. Say you have to go away for a week and you give a friend a key so she can take care of the cats while you are away. Unfortunately, your friend is not reliable. As a result, your cats are not cared for and the animal welfare office finds out about it. The officials might even have to come in and take the cats to a shelter while you are not home. Animal welfare will hold you responsible for the care of your cats—even if you are away and think you made proper arrangements for them. Therefore, always be very careful and make sure your cats are continuously cared for no matter what.

The second legal issue deals not with health and sanitary conditions, but rather with the total number of cats you have. A number of townships and counties scattered across the US and Canada have enforced capitation laws. These laws set a maximum limit on the number of pets any resident may have in one home. That limit applies even if you really can take care of twice the allowed number.

The most common capitation limit is ten. This usually applies to the total number of pets—if you have dogs as well as cats, you have to add them in, too. Before you provide a home to more than a few cats, you should check with your township (or city) and county government to make sure that you are not in an area with a capitation rule. If you are, you must stop at the number the law dictates.

A related issue is any limit on pets set by your landlord, if you rent. Even if your landlord "winks" at you having several cats when your lease specifies no cats or just one cat, that kind of approval does not protect you forever. Unless you have a signed document from the landlord allowing you to keep the number of cats you actually have, you can be evicted for breaking this rule, or the landlord can refuse to renew your lease unless you abide by his rules.

GETTING ALONG WITH YOUR NEIGHBORS

When you have cats, no matter how many, they must all be kept inside. A cat that spends *any* time outside, even "just in the yard," has a much shorter average life span than a cat that spends all of her life indoors. Also, if any of your cats go outside, you may create problems with your neighbors. Cats pay no attention to boundaries. If let outside, they can easily go into your neighbor's yard, onto their porch, or even into their house. There, they can do damage: scratches on painted steps, runs in screens, attacks on small birds, and messes in the shrubs. This kind of cat activity can quickly change a good neighbor into a bad one.

Talk to your neighbors. Let them know you have "some" or a "batch" of cats. If any of the cats might manage to get

Cats pay no attention to boundaries. A cat that continually trespasses on your neighbor's property can quickly turn a good neighbor into an annoyed neighbor.

Multiple-cat owners have to be extra careful to keep litter odors from becoming offensive.

outside, let your neighbor know which cats are yours, so they can call you to retrieve them if necessary and so they do not blame your indoor calico for what a free-roaming brown tabby is doing to their bird bath. If the cats do not ever go outside, tell your neighbors you do not let them out, so you do not get the blame for someone who is much less responsible.

What else should you do? If you have a friend who helps you with the cats or a cat-sitter who has a key to your home, give your neighbors that person's telephone number. If you are not around, the neighbors may become concerned about the welfare of your cats. If you do not give them a number, the only thing they can do is call animal welfare or do nothing at all.

Make sure that you appreciate the fact that a group of cats does indeed bother some people. But if they do not see—or smell—the cats, then people do not become concerned. Therefore, do not store cat food cases or bags of fresh litter where they are visible to neighbors from the street. Keeping them out of sight is just being polite. That also means you must be very fastidious in disposing of the cat litter (or other cat box filler) that you use, as well as things like empty cat food cans and food bags.

First, never just dispose of any used litter or litter substitute on your property, even if it is made of something degradable, like wood fibers. If you do want to use such materials in your garden, make sure that the label says you can, and follow the instructions. Then take all of the waste materials out of the substances before using them. The solid and liquid cat wastes they hold will produce very offensive and strong odors for a long time. In fact, depending on the prevailing breezes, you may not smell it now—but your unhappy neighbor might.

Second, put all used litter and cat waste products into a strong, sealed container and keep it sealed. Do the same for all food containers of any sort. Because litter can get very heavy, you should use a container with wheels so you can easily take it out to be picked up. Another hint: Be nice to your trash hauler. Put the litter and waste in a sealed plastic bag in the trash can. That makes it less likely to produce strong odors when the can is emptied and also lessens the chance that litter will spill out.

If your community recycles cans, make very sure that the cat food cans are completely rinsed out. If not, you are creating an attraction for free-

Spaying or neutering will reduce your pet's risk of getting some life-threatening diseases. It will also help prevent some behavioral problems, such as spraying.

roaming cats as well as for raccoons and rodents when the cans are at curbside— plus the rodents and insects that may be uninvited guests when the cans are still in your home.

THE NEED FOR IMMEDIATE SPAYING AND NEUTERING

There are several very good reasons why you should spay all female cats and neuter all male cats as soon as possible.

First, it is the only responsible way to proceed. Unless you are a professional breeder of pedigreed cats, you should not be breeding cats for any reason. From a health point of view, your cats are better off being spayed or neutered. For example, if a female is spayed before she ever has a heat cycle, her risk of mammary cancer decreases almost to the point of being nonexistent. Furthermore, by doing this, you will not contribute to the overpopulation of cats, particularly free-roaming homeless cats.

Second, by spaying or neutering a cat sooner rather than later, you avoid the problem of an accidental litter. No matter what anyone tells you, you cannot be certain that an unneutered cat will not breed. Cats can begin to breed as young as four or five months old and can continue being able to breed for ten or more years.

Third, by spaying and neutering all of your cats, you make it easier for them to adapt to each other and to live with each other. Even if you do not have any whole males, for example, having two or more whole females going into heat can cause a noticeable negative change in the atmosphere in your home for all of your cats.

Fourth, after being spayed and neutered, your cats are significantly less likely to try to run away due to being attracted to the dangerous outside by other cats in heat. Also, they are less likely to attract free-roaming or feral whole cats to the environs of your home, a situation that can cause additional problems for you and all of your cats.

Finally, if a cat is spayed or neutered before he or she begins to spray, the animal is very unlikely to develop that bad habit. As for cats that come to you already spraying, spaying or neutering them will make it easier for them to stop that unwelcome behavior.

Unless you are a professional breeder of pedigreed cats, it is irresponsible to breed cats for any reason. Have your cats spayed or neutered as soon as they are old enough so you do not contribute to pet overpopulation.

When you see just how agile cats can be, you quickly realize that the home environment, designed and decorated for humans, must be adapted when you have multiple cats in the household in order for the humans and the cats to exist in harmony. Cats need to jump, scratch, run, and play. They need room to get away from each other and to take a nap. They need room to hide from each other in order to mount an ambush on a fellow cat. They need room to wrestle and chase their toys. They need a very safe environment that is free of poisons as well as attractive large and small items that might choke or injure them.

ADAPTING THE ENVIRONMENT FOR MULTIPLE CATS

When you have a multiple-cat household, you will want to adapt the house for the cats' comfort as well as for your own. While you *can* live with both multiple cats and beautiful china, everyone in your household might feel much less uneasy if some modifications are made. You must always remember that your home is the cats' environment as well. It is their "jungle," and everything in your home is their property, from their point of view.

When you buy upholstered furniture, run your fingernail along it carefully to see how vulnerable the fabric is to cat claws. Do the same with wooden furniture. Even though you should be clipping your cat's claws routinely, the nail of a cat is sharp, and some furniture is very fragile and easily scarred. Therefore, you will want to make sure that all your furniture is sturdy enough to take the jumping, playing, and general activity level of your cats.

Take into account the size of your cats when you look at furniture. Big cats and delicate tables do not make a good combination. Likewise, white, long-haired cats and a black velvet sofa will keep you so busy picking up cat hair that you won't have time to enjoy the pleasure of your cats' company. If you have very fragile items, you might

Cats are agile, athletic animals that need to jump, scratch, run, and play. The cat owner's house must be adapted to suit these needs.

While it's certainly possible to live with both cats *and* expensive breakables, it's probably not a good idea unless the cats are extremely well trained.

want to consider buying a cabinet with glass doors on the front so that you can enjoy your items as well as your cats.

While you are adapting your own environment to be shared with your cats, you will also want to give them some items that are truly theirs. Cat trees with surfaces that your cats can scratch all they want are absolutely critical in creating a mutually happy environment. To attract your cats to their trees, spray them regularly with catnip spray. Since there will be quiet times when one or more of the cats will want some time alone, small houses or cat trees with holes for them to hide in will be most welcome.

Your cats will also enjoy their own soft, fabric beds. Watch your cats find their favorite spot and then place a cat bed there. All cat "furniture" and beds should

Your cats will appreciate scratching posts and cat trees—the bigger and more elaborate, the better.

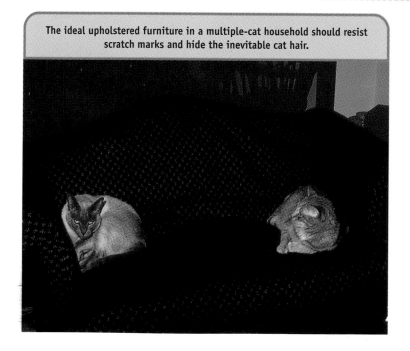

The ideal upholstered furniture in a multiple-cat household should resist scratch marks and hide the inevitable cat hair.

be washable with a deodorizer and disinfectant. Don't forget plenty of toys. If you don't provide enough toys, the cats may very well make a toy of everything else in the house.

If you have one or more older cats in your multiple-cat household, you will want to make certain that this older cat can still comfortably access all the areas she has enjoyed during her life. In order to accomplish this, make a little "staircase" for her. This can consist of something as simple as a small stool that enables her to take two steps to get where she used to go when she could jump comfortably on her own. Be certain that there is a stair to the litter box that the older cat uses as well, especially if you use the larger litter boxes with the higher sides. You can accomplish this easily by using a small litter box turned upside down next to the large litter box. This provides a step for your older cat. Also be certain that you get a chance to watch your older cat eat and drink. If the cat has any problem getting close enough to her dish to eat or drink, you can easily elevate it for her convenience.

CATPROOFING YOUR HOME FOR SAFETY

Catproofing is the process of making your home safe for your cats. The best way to begin catproofing your home is to get down to the level of your cats. If you can, literally crawl on the floor throughout the house and find out how things look from that angle.

If you were small enough, could you get under the sofa and hide there? Is it safe under there? A recliner can be a very dangerous, even deadly, piece of furniture if a cats hides under it.

If you were a cat, could you pull open the cabinets and get to potentially poisonous cleaning solutions? A determined cat can work until she manages to pull a cabinet door open, just because she wants to see what is behind the door. If your cats try to do this, you can put a better latch on the door or you can add a childproof latch to the cabinet.

Is there wicker that a cat might scratch apart, swallow, and injure herself with? Yes, this can happen. Cats will try to taste anything and may

For a cat that wants to be alone, a cat house is the perfect hideaway.

gnaw on broken wicker.

Are there plants that your cats can get to and graze on? Even if you make certain that the only plants you have around are safe for cats to eat, one of your cats may see the plants as a very attractive salad bar and gorge herself on them.

Are there electrical cords in a tangle? If so, they can also tangle around and trap a cat

or a kitten. Electrical cords should be taped together or put into a hollow tube.

Once you have checked the low spots, go back and check the high spots. Cats climb and jump. They can easily get on top of appliances and cabinets. Is it safe up there for them? Can they slip and fall into danger if they don't land properly? Despite their

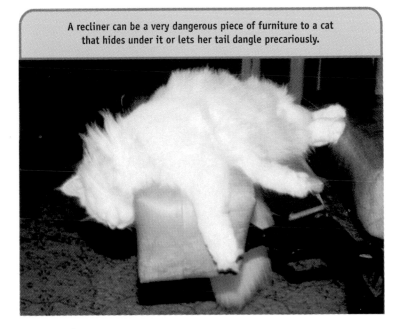

A recliner can be a very dangerous piece of furniture to a cat that hides under it or lets her tail dangle precariously.

The home is full of potential trouble spots for a cat. In a sewing area, pins, needles, thread, and the sewing machine itself are all dangerous temptations.

natural grace, cats can slip, and while they usually land on their feet, an unexpected fall can still cause injury.

Kittens are a very special problem. To kittens, everything has to go into the mouth, and they seem to be unafraid of anything. They can also get into areas that bigger cats cannot get into. With their undeveloped muscles, they don't have the

grace or agility of an adult cat, so they might not be able to get out from tight places as easily as they got in.

Older cats, on the other hand, tend to slow down and stay in their favorite spots for the most part. Older cats will want a nice place to get away and be by themselves at times. However, older cats may not be able to reach these

special places as easily as they have in the past. Therefore, they may need for you to make a set of steps for them to use to get up to their favorite places so they do not hurt themselves in the attempt.

Once you have catproofed your home, you must still remain alert to potential danger. You must always keep your cats in mind when you decorate for any occasion. The holidays are critical when it comes to catproofing. Lights on a Christmas tree mean loose electric cords, and loose electric cords can be very dangerous to cats. This is also true when it comes to garlands and small, dangling objects that attract cats to Christmas trees. Check every ornament you put on the tree and make very certain that it will not hurt your cat if it becomes a cat toy. Naturally, breakable ornaments should never be used. You must also be very careful with candles. Keep them up where the cats can't reach them or jump up to them, and use a hurricane lamp to cover them. Never burn candles in a room if you are not present. Remember that holidays are not the only time to check your catproofing attempts. You will want to be very careful at any celebration, such as a birthday party.

From time to time, you may have people in your home to redecorate, repair, or paint a room. Be certain to keep your cats away from the work area. In addition, because many of these renovations bring in new odors, your cats will have to readjust to these new smells. Cats can smell odors that we humans cannot, so

To be safe, make sure that your houseplants are completely nontoxic to cats.

just because you can't smell the new paint does not mean that your cats can't. Expect a degree of curiosity and a bit of commotion as your cats get used to the new smells and new objects in your home.

CLEANING

One of the most important chores you have in the multiple-cat household is to keep the premises clean and sanitary. A house with multiple cats should still smell like a house and not like a stable. First, you will want to make sure you have enough litter boxes for the cats in your home—at least one per cat, if possible. While you should scoop all the boxes daily, you should also dump at least one of them completely each day and wash

Kitties love to climb trees, and the sparkly Christmas tree is no exception. Be extra careful to catproof your house during the holidays.

There are cat-engaging, recreational activity centers on the market that are designed so the cat owner can build, take apart, or add on to expand from a single level to an endless floor to ceiling playground. Photo courtesy of Kitty Playland.

that box well using a deodorizer and a disinfectant. You will need to do this even if you use litter box liners. Cats can eventually scratch little holes in even the sturdiest liners, and litter dust and urine can seep beneath the liner. You may also want to put a solid or automatic aerosol deodorizer in the area where each litter box is kept to keep the air fresh for you and your family.

You must also clean up any accidents immediately and use a deodorizer in that area. This also holds true when one of your cats happens to throw up a hairball and leaves it out for you. You do not want the hairball turned into a cat toy or swallowed by another cat.

You should vacuum your home frequently and be certain to wash cat beds regularly as well. In addition, the regular use of the new

Unless you live in a barn, your multiple-cat household should smell like a house and not like a stable.

commercial products that clean odors out of fabrics is extremely useful when it comes to keeping the multiple-cat household clean and fresh-smelling for you.

PURCHASING AND STORING SUPPLIES

In the multiple-cat household, you will, of course, use up food and litter much faster than in a single-cat household, but careful planning may help you keep the costs from rising too much.

Think about what you are feeding your cats. Do they eat canned food, dry food, or both? Some cats tend to eat only canned food, while others gravitate to dry food. Do you know which cat does what? How much of each type of food do they eat? When you tally all of this, you can estimate how much of each type of food you have to buy to feed your cats for ten days to two weeks, a good guideline.

Also determine what foods your cats will eat. Cats have developed a reputation for being finicky. Some of them really are, but there are many reasons why cats seem to ignore food you put out. Do not assume that if they have stopped eating a particular cat food, you must switch to something else.

Most people do not know that cats do not eat on the same schedule we do. The average cat does not eat every day. In fact, a cat tends to eat about five or six days out of seven. So, from time to time, your cats will seem to eat less. It is often just that they may be off-cycle.

Sometimes cats do seem to go off food, usually more often with canned food than with dry food. Often it is not the flavor, but rather the brand itself. If neglecting food occurs, stop feeding that brand, and shift to another brand you have tested. This means you should have previously tried small amounts of different canned foods to see which ones your cats will eat. Buy several different brands to keep on hand.

Cats can become very finicky, but only if we let them. Cats, being as intelligent as they are, quickly learn that you can be manipulated. If a cat prefers one food and you give another, she may try ignoring the food. If you then make a big fuss and give her back the first food, is that cat finicky or are you just well trained?

Once you determine what the cats will eat, purchase a

Cats keep *themselves* clean, but you are responsible for the rest of the house.

If your cat is refusing to eat her food, try a different kind that you know she likes.

variety of foods to keep on hand. Cans may be stored anywhere that they are not exposed to extremes of heat or cold. That means if you have the space in a semi-finished basement, you may be able to store cans there. If you have enough room, consider buying some or all of your cat food at a warehouse club. There, you will find canned foods sold in cases containing from 24 to 48 cans. First make sure that these are brands that your cats will eat *and* that the prices are really low. While warehouse clubs usually have better prices on the cans of food they carry, aggressive seasonal sales and coupon offers can often mean that a local grocery chain is a better place to buy much of that food.

Dry foods should be handled the same way. That is, identify two or three brands that your cats will eat. Then consider buying the dry foods in bulk. These foods come in bags of up to 40

Some cats tend to eat only canned food, while others gravitate to dry food. Some kitties even like dog food! Plan carefully and buy the foods you use in advance.

pounds. However, you must be very careful in storing bags of dry food. Not only do you want to avoid extremes of temperature, you *must* avoid areas where moisture can build up or where your cats (or dogs, if you have them) can get at the bags. Careful storage is necessary even for a resealed bag. Once a bag is opened, it should be used until it is finished. Until then, it should be stored in a safe, dry location where it will not attract cats or pests.

If you need special foods for your cats, see if a pet supply store will give you a discount for buying in bulk. Also, if you have to buy a special diet from your veterinarian, make sure that you know both the prices and the amount that you may feed. If you have a concern about the costs of such food, feel free to ask your veterinarian if you can use another brand or can adapt a commercial food for your cat's particular needs.

Litter, whether clay or

Those comfy cat beds can collect a lot of hair and dirt over time. Make sure to wash them frequently.

clumping, should be stored in an area from which you can easily move it to fill the litter boxes. You should also change your litter boxes where you can avoid too much dust. For many households, this means that the litter should be stored in a garage and the boxes filled

there. This measure will keep you from bringing a source of dust into your home and also means that the bags of litter do not have to be moved too far or too often.

Buying litter in bulk sizes at warehouse clubs is often a very cost-effective way to proceed. As with the food, the bag sizes are large. Clay litter is usually sold only in 40- or 50-pound bags, which can be hard to handle. Clumping litter comes in containers ranging in size from 20 to 40 pounds. Again, always check the unit prices on all litter products you buy. You may be surprised to find that the national high-volume retail stores sometimes sell litter at a lower price than do nearby warehouse clubs.

If buying in bulk by yourself is not an option, try to find another cat lover who will split the cases of food and bags of food and litter with you. That will let each of you save money without having to store as much.

The more cats you have, the more litter you will need. Buying litter in bulk from warehouse clubs can save you money.

SELECTING THE DIET

No matter what cat food you use, make certain that it says on the can or bag that it meets the American Association of Feed Control Officials (AAFCO) standards and provides complete and balanced nutrition for the growth and maintenance of cats. In the multiple-cat household, you will face all kinds of dietary issues, including dealing with overweight cats, very young cats and kittens, older cats, and cats with special dietary needs.

The problem that faces most of us with multiple cats is making certain that the cats do not get too fat. This is especially true if the cats eat together or if a bowl or feeder of crunchy cat food is available at

Cats that are particularly prone to hairballs may benefit from one of the new foods designed to help prevent them.

Dry kitten food is enriched with additional nutrients and comes in smaller pieces than food designed for adults.

If your cat is overweight, try feeding her a "light" or "senior" version of the dry food she already enjoys.

all times. If an overweight cat is a problem for you, try adding green beans to canned food to provide bulk without adding calories or fat. When it comes to dry food, there are many brands available now that feature a lower calorie or "light" version of the food or a "senior" version that is also lower in calories and easier to digest. This food can be mixed in with the other dry food you are feeding or it can be fed by itself. Dry food can also be added to canned food to extend it.

Many people wonder if it is necessary to buy a canned food made specifically for kittens. If the canned food you normally feed is labeled "balanced for growth," you are perfectly safe feeding this food to kittens and young cats. The difference you may find will be in connection with dry food for adults as opposed to that for kittens. Dry food comes in

A round, stainless-steel dish that is designed to feed a litter of puppies is perfect for feeding canned food in the multiple-cat household.

all sorts of shapes and sizes. Some of the dry food pieces may be too big or hard for a kitten to crunch. Kitten food, on the other hand, comes in very small pieces. If you cannot find or prefer

not to use dry kitten food, you can buy dry food that comes in small pieces or pieces that have holes in them. You may also feed kittens a dry food mixed with a small amount of water. All of these measures make dry food easier for a kitten to eat.

When it comes to adult cats, you may want to make sure that you feed a diet designed to help prevent dental problems. You can do this by mixing dry dental diets into the mix of dry foods you provide. These diets, available through your veterinarian or at grocery and feed stores, come in larger-size pieces. When you first introduce these dental foods, you might find that the pieces of food become toys for a short period of time, but the cats will adapt to this diet rather quickly. The dental diets are supposed to help clean the tartar off the teeth of the

It is always a good idea to have a cat-attractive substitute for your furniture around the house that satisfies your cat's instinctual need to scratch, climb and play. Photo courtesy of Kitty Playland.

cats. They work in the manner of gnawing on a bone.

While we usually don't think of giving bones to cats, many of them love scraping the meat off a cooked lamb leg bone or a large cooked ham or beef leg bone. Scraping their teeth against the large, hard bone also helps cats to get the teeth clean. Of course, you never want to give cats chicken or turkey bones, which might splinter, or small meat bones that could cause them to choke.

In addition to dental diets, there are also dry foods available for cats that get hairballs. These diets are available at large pet stores.

Sometimes you will find that a certain food will cause your cats to pass loose stools or even suffer from diarrhea. This does not mean that the food is bad. It could be because the brand of food they are eating is very high in available protein and your cat just can't tolerate that sort of diet. Just eliminate this food from the diet. Cats like variety, so varying the food is not a problem for them.

Cats that eat a balanced diet do not really need supplements. However, cats that are ill will do better with a vitamin supplement. If your cats aren't eating at all, you may use a liquid vitamin or a paste made especially for this situation.

FEEDING YOUR CATS

If your cats all get along well, it is easy to feed them together from large dishes. One type of dish that is handy for multiple cats is one that is designed to feed a litter of puppies. This is a large round dish that allows the cats to line up along the edge of it. For serving hard cat food, gravity feeders are popular and readily available. These come apart for ease of cleaning.

If you have older cats, they can be segregated in a private feeding area and fed diets created especially for the senior cat. These diets consist of both canned and dry food. Dry senior food may also be mixed into the general dish without interfering with the nutritional needs of the remainder of the cats.

If you have a cat whose diet must be controlled, usually for medical reasons, this cat should be fed in a separate area away from the other cats. The cat food should be taken away from the other cats before all the cats are once again allowed to mingle with each other. If the special-needs cat appears unhappy with this arrangement, perhaps you can have another cat that is a special friend of hers eat with her and keep her company. Most special diets will not harm a cat that doesn't really need the diet, as long as she gets at least one nutritionally complete meal each day.

Clean, fresh water is critical to good health for your cats.

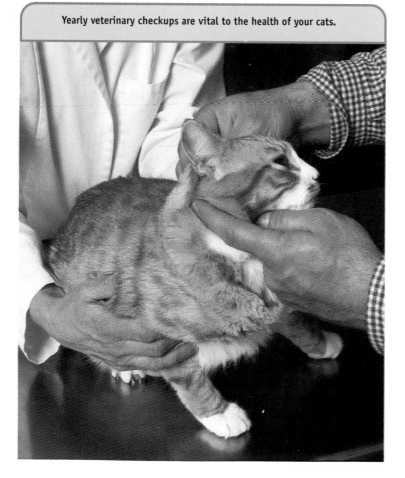

Yearly veterinary checkups are vital to the health of your cats.

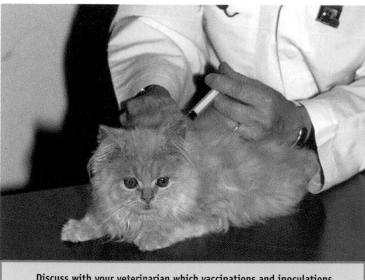

Discuss with your veterinarian which vaccinations and inoculations your cats require. A rabies vaccination may be required by law.

which are diseases that can kill cats. There are also vaccines that claim to protect against ringworm and "kennel cough," which may also strike and spread through a multiple-cat environment. You should discuss these optional inoculations with your veterinarian and be guided by that advice.

Even though your cats are indoors, they can still get fleas. You, your visitors, or your cat-sitter may bring fleas in from outdoors on clothing, or they may get into your house through the little invisible cracks around almost all doors and windows.

Fleas are a terrible parasite. They can cause more damage to cats than just a loss of fur due to scratching. Fleas transmit tapeworms to cats and, in case of an infestation, can even cause anemia in a cat.

Today, flea control is very simple. There are many products available from your veterinarian that can eliminate

Be certain that the water dish you use is big enough to provide adequately for all of your cats. It is often necessary to use several dishes so that all of your cats can get to a water bowl easily.

When you have many cats, you may find that a water dish is also used for play. Do not be surprised if you find a toy carefully deposited in the water dish. If your cats are this playful, you will want to check the water dish frequently during the day to make certain that it is full of clean water—and nothing else.

MONITORING HEALTH IN A GROUP

Even though your cats are kept strictly in an indoor environment, they still need yearly veterinary checks and inoculations with yearly booster shots. These vaccines protect your cats from the most common contagious diseases affecting cats. In addition, the state where you live may require that your cats

receive a rabies vaccination from a veterinarian licensed in your state.

In addition to the routine inoculations, there are some optional vaccines. These tend to be for contagious diseases such as feline leukemia and feline infectious peritonitis,

Prevent fleas from becoming a problem by regularly grooming your cat with a flea comb and using prescription medication if necessary.

fleas on your cats. Some of these remedies are oral and some of them are topical. They may have to be used several times during the flea season, but they can save your cats from this terrible parasite and make you comfortable knowing you are taking care of your cats. Flea control is something you should undertake before there is a problem. Your veterinarian can assist you when it comes to deciding which kind of flea control is best for you and your cats.

There are other parasites such as ear and body mites that can be passed rapidly from one cat to another, but most of these parasites must be treated by your veterinarian. Preventive care, which you practice when dealing with flea control, can keep these parasites out of the life of your cats.

You will want to brush your cats every day whether they are short-haired cats or long-haired cats. When you do this,

It's easy for diseases to spread from one cat to another when they are in close contact. Separate any sick cats from the others to prevent a mini-epidemic.

also use this time as an opportunity to give each cat a bit of a physical examination. Check your cats' ears. Are they clean? If there is a brownish discharge, gently clean the ears

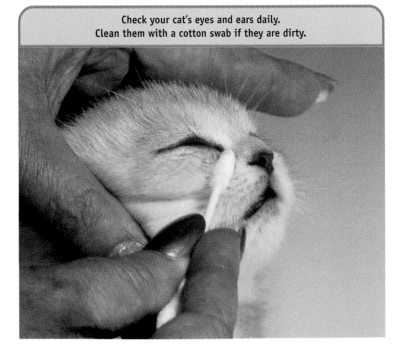

Check your cat's eyes and ears daily. Clean them with a cotton swab if they are dirty.

with a cotton swab and perhaps an ear cleanser made specifically for cats. Do this very carefully but completely.

Next, check your cat's eyes. Are they clean, with no tearing? They should be bright and clear. Some cats will have a weepy discharge in their eyes due to allergies. While this can be helped by using a natural-tear eye drop or a mild eye drop for allergies, you will want to check with your veterinarian before you put anything in your cats' eyes.

Check the cats' mouths and teeth as well. If the gums are red and a cat has bad breath, it may be time to schedule that annual teeth cleaning.

Next, run your hands all over your cat. Concentrate especially on the cheeks and neck. You are feeling to make certain that the lymph nodes are normal in size. If they are swollen, take the cat to your veterinarian to be checked as soon as you can.

When you need to separate your cats,
a cage or carrier is a necessity.

THE NEED FOR ISOLATION AND SEPARATE QUARTERS

When living in a multiple-cat household, you must expect to deal with medical and other problems. Some of them may be emergencies; others will be chronic. In addition to having the proper first aid supplies, litter, food, etc. on hand, you should plan for the possibility that you will have to separate one or more cats from the others.

For example, if one of your cats develops an upper respiratory infection, you should separate her while she is being treated so that she does not make other cats sick. For the sick cat, you will need a room in which she can live where she will not have contact with other cats. If the cat is very sick, you may need to set up a cage in the room to confine her. You do this so that she does not hide from you under a bed or behind a bookcase. If she is weak, you

are also helping her conserve her energy by placing her food, bedding, water, and litter close at hand.

You may need to separate otherwise healthy cats. Why? If one has to be placed on a special diet, whether for weight loss or to control a

medical problem, you will have to have a place to feed her. You also need to keep her from eating the regular food you give to the rest of the cats. If you do not leave food out, all you need is to have a large cage where you confine a cat to feed her separately from all of the others. When the cats have finished eating, you simply release the cat on the special diet.

Consider where you will have the following. You will need:

• A cage or carrier to temporarily house a cat while she is being given a special meal or for ease in administering medication.

• A separate room in which to house cats, either temporarily or permanently, that need to be separated from the others because of medical or physical reasons, as well as for the purpose of controlling aggressive behavior.

• A large cage in a

A cage will help a very sick cat to recover by forcing her to conserve her energy. It will also keep germs from spreading to the other cats.

Multiple-cat owners should make a special effort to find the perfect veterinarian. The veterinarian should be able to address the special needs of each cat—not to mention those of the owner.

separate room in which to confine ill cats so they can be treated, while protecting the rest of the cats from a contagious illness or condition.

DEALING WITH VETERINARIANS

Establishing a Relationship

If you do not have a veterinarian with whom you have a good longtime relationship, you must select a veterinarian with whom you can establish such a relationship, and with whom you can work closely. You will quickly find that your veterinarian is the most important person in your cats' lives—other than you.

It may take some time to find the veterinarian you want. We as multiple-cat owners can be very demanding. When we go to our veterinarian's office, we want to be seen immediately, and we want to have the time to discuss how this ill cat and her care relate to the entire household, no matter how busy the doctor might be. We may do a little of our own veterinary care, and some of us, unfortunately, may hesitate to go to the veterinarian until a cat is quite ill. We may also want the veterinarian to allow us to pay our bills over a period of time. We may need house calls by our veterinarian; and because we care deeply about our cats, we never hesitate to call our veterinarian in the middle of the night if we have a problem.

The most important aspect in your selection of a veterinarian is not the physical office, but the veterinarian himself. Consider the following in selecting a veterinarian:

- Will you be able to build a relationship with this veterinarian?
- Will you be able to talk to him and will you trust him when he prescribes a drug for your cat or recommends an operation?
- Will you follow his advice on techniques for dealing with your cats?

All these aspects of your relationship are critical. You never want to feel that you did something that harmed one of your cats because you felt you could not ask your veterinarian about something.

The ideal veterinarian for a multiple-cat household is one who has some experience or training in kennel or cattery management. Because of this training, he will understand how to care for several cats that are living in the same household. He must also know about the spread and control of infectious and contagious diseases, as well as about fungi and parasites, because a multiple-cat household can be very vulnerable if any of these are accidentally introduced into the household. He should be an expert in preventive medicine, because you would rather have proper techniques employed to prevent a problem instead of waiting until that problem is at hand and then trying to treat it.

Make an appointment to meet with a veterinarian you are considering using so that you can interview him. During the interview, you should ask about subjects that are critical to you, such as:

- What has been his training?
- Has he had previous experience working with multiple-cat households like yours?
- Can you see his facilities for boarding cats that must be at the veterinarian's overnight?
- Does he release males that have been neutered or females that have been spayed the same day they have had their surgery?
- Who covers his practice at night and on the weekends?

The answers to these

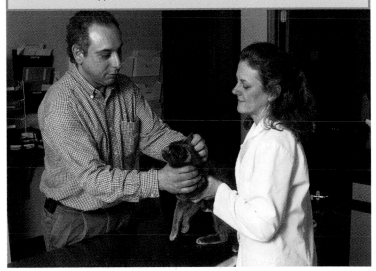

Interview your potential veterinarian carefully beforehand or at the first appointment. Feel free to ask for references.

Some multiple-cat owners may wish to ask their veterinarian for training in giving inoculations. This can save some money and prevent stress to the cats.

questions will help you decide whether or not you will be able to work with the veterinarian you are interviewing.

Feel free to ask any veterinarian you are interviewing for references. Then call those people whose names he gives you and ask them how they feel about that particular veterinarian. Have they had any problems with him? Was he available when they needed him? Does he listen to them?

Maintaining that Relationship

Once you have selected a veterinarian and have established a good relationship, never abuse that relationship. Realize that while your veterinarian has a friendly relationship with you, his patients are your cats.

Veterinarians are limited by law from prescribing medications without examining a sick animal. Your veterinarian may be able to make an exception to this if you have a good relationship, he knows the cat, and he knows that you are very careful in describing the physical signs of illnesses or problems with your cats. In

states where rabies inoculations are mandatory, your veterinarian must inoculate all your cats for rabies unless he feels there is a legitimate health reason to avoid doing so. Responsible pet owners never put their veterinarian in a compromising position.

Special Needs

Once you have established a good relationship with your veterinarian, make sure that you try to make it work as well as your veterinarian is trying to do. For example, you may want to ask your veterinarian if he will make house calls. These calls

may be made annually so he can give all of your cats required inoculations, or they may be to necessary to enable him to treat several cats at once. If he can treat your cats but is limited as to what he can do on a house call, accept that. Work with your veterinarian.

You may want to ask your veterinarian if you can be trained so that you can take better care of your cats. For example, if you have training, you may be able to give your cats their regular inoculations, other than the one against rabies. Not only will inoculating them yourself save you money (even though you have to buy the drugs), it will put less stress on your cats. If inoculated at home they do not have to travel to the veterinarian's office for their annual shots.

If a medical or physical condition means special care for one of your cats, ask your veterinarian if you yourself can provide some or all of that care. If you can, your veterinarian will be happy to work with you. If your veterinarian feels that a treatment is difficult or dangerous for you to do, respect that decision.

Your choice of veterinarian will be particularly important if you ever have to board your cat at the vet's office overnight.

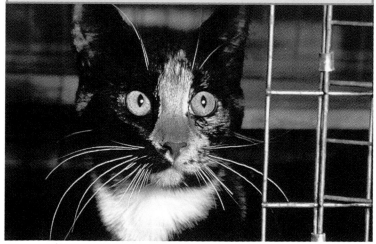

BEHAVIORAL ISSUES

THE HIERARCHY

As we noted earlier, your cats all live in a hierarchy in your home. The existence of that hierarchy is one of the most important factors in how your cats behave, both individually and as a group. Unlike in a single cat household, in a multiple-cat household your cats are constantly trying to relate not only to each other cat, but also to combinations of other cats. That means that the owner of a multiple-cat household needs to understand how to deal with issues such as aggression and shyness in ways that a single-cat owner does not. It also means that the responsible multiple-cat owner has to move very quickly to avoid having what seems to be a small problem escalate into a major one.

Always keep this speed of dealing with a problem in mind and try to think of ways to keep the entire cat colony in balance. For example, daily play with a toy that a number of your cats like to chase and attack diverts their attention from other cats that do not want to join in. This kind of activity keeps the entire colony more in harmony.

PLAY

It is always so much fun just sitting around watching your cats at play. You can just imagine what is going on in their minds when they chase each other, ambush and wrestle with each other, and chase their toys. Playtime is when you realize that you are lucky to be sharing a space that is obviously theirs and theirs alone. You are the spectator. Play is important for all cats because it exercises their muscles and burns off the calories they consume. It keeps your cats in excellent physical condition

The hierarchy of the cats in your home is an important factor in their behavior patterns.

A fishing pole-type cat toy is very popular with both cats and their owners. They require very little effort by the human and provide much entertainment for the feline.

and provides the enjoyment that they need so much.

You can play with them by throwing their toys for them to chase. Try buying some interactive toys that you can

both enjoy. Some of the toys that are fun for both owners and cats are those that look like a rod or fishing pole with a toy on the end of it. You can sit comfortably and gently

Play is important for all cats because it exercises their muscles and burns off the calories they consume. More importantly, though, it's fun!

toss the toy over the heads of your cats and let them try to catch it. There are also mechanical toys that run on batteries. These are generally little mice that run around the floor with the use of a hand control and mice that run around a plastic ring.

Most cat toys are very safe for supervised play. However, you will want to be careful not to let your cats play with toys that have long strings that may entangle them. You may want to remove any small, decorative pieces of plastic or small bells on cat toys if you have young kittens around.

While kittens seem to be the most active players, an adult cat should have several sessions each day of active play. An older cat will probably not be as active, play as frequently, or play for long periods of time. In fact, sometimes when a younger cat tries to get an older cat to play, the older cat may hiss or swat at the youngster. This is not unusual.

ADJUSTING TO NEW ARRIVALS

When you bring a new cat or kitten into a multiple-cat household, you must realize that the established cats will react. That is because this new cat, however cute, is a stranger, and is perceived as coming into *their* home and tribe. The first step toward keeping the peace in your home is to understand and accept this. You cannot make one cat accept another by shouting or using a squirt gun. Rather, you must work to let both the established cats and the newcomer understand that the change is permanent and nonthreatening.

The first step should be to

confine the new arrival. Confining her does not mean caging her. It means putting her into one room and keeping her there. You do not want the new arrival to be overwhelmed by having access to the entire house, nor do you want her to have to deal with the other cats right away.

In the room where the cat is confined, use your regular food dishes and litter boxes, so the arrival gets used to them. If the new cat came with a favorite bed or toy, use this along with your own bedding instead of washing it right away. You want the arrival to become used to the home, the noises, the smells, the food, the bedding, and your schedule. Whenever you open up any area to the new arrival, which you should do gradually if you can, make sure you show the newcomer where the litter box is by putting her in it. You will also want to show the new cat where the food and water is.

You may desire at the same time to bring out something belonging to the new arrival for the resident cats to smell, such as the plate of food from which she just ate. Do not bring out bedding, or the established cats may relieve themselves on it to show that they are still in charge.

If possible, choose a room for the arrival where the existing cats can paw playfully with her under the door. That makes the arrival seem more familiar. Over a week or so, introduce the arrival to more and more of the house and to the cats in each room.

Because cats identify friends from foes and the familiar from the unfamiliar by scent, take advantage of that. Make sure that the arrival smells like you. Hold her and pet her. A good trick is to make use of a scent your cats associate with you, such as aftershave, cologne, perfume, or even a scented powder. You do this by using the scent yourself. Then place a very small amount of this scent on the new arrival, between the ears and on the back of the head. Then apply the scent to the rest of the cats. Your goal is to make the arrival seem familiar by scent.

Even with tricks like this, the new arrival may have problems settling in. That is because every group of cats has its own hierarchy, and the new arrival is going to have to find her place in the one in your home. There may be hissing and batting. You will just have to tolerate a bit of this and realize that it really will stop once the new

Ideally, cat owners should play with their cats several times each day whether they are adult cats or kittens.

Toys with balls or mice that run around a ring allow cats to play by themselves for hours.

arrival is integrated into the household. Of course, if at all possible, make sure the arrival has been spayed or neutered *before* bringing him or her in. A whole cat may find it more difficult to fit into your home than will one that has been altered. In fact, if you wait and have the new arrival altered after she comes into your home, you may find that you have to reintroduce her to the rest of the cats.

Make sure the new arrival comes to the regular feeding spots. Bring her to the spot if necessary at first. Try to create some group activities, such as group grooming or playing with a flying toy. Your goal is to have all of the cats

accept the arrival. Within a short time, it will seem as if the newcomer has been there forever.

In the rare case where the arrival does not fit in, you may have to make adjustments—such as limiting a cat's access to certain rooms—to accommodate a new hierarchy. This is why knowing how much space you have and how you can use it is critical to the owner in a multiple-cat household. However, this permanent rearranging should be a last resort.

AGGRESSION AND CAT "FIGHTS"

To the uninitiated, cats seem to fight more than other animals do. Actually, what we call fighting is more often one of several other circumstances:

• It is just the cats as a group playing at being feral creatures, a form of both amusement and training.

• It involves an older cat teaching a younger cat how to hunt, even if they are merely stalking a catnip toy.

• It may be a function of the cats sorting out among themselves who is on top of the cat hierarchy in the house.

The first two situations are perfectly normal. In fact, you should encourage active play by your cats with each other and with you. In addition to the obvious health benefits, it may help to reduce tension and potential aggressive behavior among the cats that play together.

It is only the last situation (regarding hierarchy) that should concern you. Above all, you cannot change the

Make sure that the new arrival smells like you and like the other cats by dabbing your favorite perfume or cologne on all of your furry friends before they meet.

When you bring a new cat or kitten into the house, confine her to one room for a week or so. This will make her introduction to the other cats go more smoothly.

New cats should be introduced slowly and carefully to other pets, or else the fur is likely to fly.

way the cats relate to each other, so do not just intervene if two cats seem to be fighting excessively. Rather, make sure that their claws are very well trimmed, and try to minimize the length of time that they fight. This is best accomplished by startling them. A water pistol can be really effective. It does not harm them, it is not loud, and it is inexpensive. In addition, once your cats associate it with breaking up an activity, merely reaching for it can

sometimes stop unwanted behavior. Of course, if you have to resort to the use of the water pistol, make certain to pet each cat involved in the "battle" when it is over.

In the multiple-cat household, however, even the most benign catfights can have repercussions. Some cat owners refer to these effects as the pachinko syndrome. That name comes from a popular pinball game that features a multitude of separate pinballs moving all at once. In the multiple-cat household, it refers to the situation that a fight between two cats can trigger. The fight may cause two other cats to join the fight going on, fight a new battle between themselves, or flee the scene. These sudden actions then trigger more reactions by other cats, and so on.

LAPSES IN LITTER BOX TRAINING

Every cat owner has faced or at least worried about litter box problems. A cat that stops using a litter box immediately causes a problem for her owner and in her environment. If you have only one cat, you know the culprit and usually the cause immediately, and you can try to deal with the problem at once.

In a multiple-cat household, experience has shown that the owner should use as many litter boxes as possible. Distribute them throughout the house. Try to place them in spots where there is relative quiet and never where there is cat food. Cats will not eat where they excrete.

You may find that you cannot use covered litter boxes, the type that most owners prefer. Some cats, particularly shy ones, do not

How can you tell if your cats are really fighting or just playing? To experienced cat owners, the differences are clear—snarling, hissing, laid-back ears, and genuine injuries are some of the clues.

Group play sessions with your cats are a great way to break down barriers between the long-time residents and the newcomer.

like to use them. You may have to have some boxes that are not covered.

Also, do not change the litter you use without a good reason. Cats depend on smell, and different litters smell different. A particularly finicky cat may try to avoid a litter because it has a strong, perfumed smell—probably the reason you selected it in the first place.

In a multiple-cat household, the owner must move quickly if he or she encounters any litter box problem. Above all, keep in mind that in a multiple-cat household, if one cat breaks litter box training, it may cause other cats to do likewise—almost at once. This is because what we see as improper elimination is seen by your cats as an effort to "mark territory," even if eliminating outside the box was an unpremeditated accident. With several cats, you need have only one of the other cats respond to an accident by improperly eliminating in or near the same area to have a problem

After any litter box accident, work quickly to thoroughly remove any scent in the area.

that gets worse—rapidly.

So, when there is any kind of litter box problem, do not just clean it up at once. Make sure that you work to remove *any* scent in the entire area. Not only is the scent a potential invitation for other cats to mess there, but the presence of the scent may drive some cats to go to other litter boxes or to mess elsewhere in the house. Why? The answer

is that the cat hierarchy in your home may control which cats use which litter boxes. If cat number one forces cat number two to go to cat number three's litter box, that may cause other behavior problems.

Immediately try to find out which cat triggered a box change and why. If you find out which cat is responsible, that fact may let you know why. Perhaps the problem is that one cat finds herself chased away from a more dominant cat's "personal" box. Solution? Set up another box. Perhaps the cat you have identified as the culprit may look uncomfortable when she is in or near the box. In that case, immediately try to rule out any medical or physical problem. Cats often mess outside of their litter box to draw attention to discomfort, such as a urinary tract infection. Be aware of that possibility. If the cat eliminating outside of the box is an older cat, can she easily get into the box or does she need a step to make it easier for her to get in and out of the box?

On the other hand, you may not determine any reason

It can be difficult to determine the reason for litter problems, but sometimes they are related to the location of the box. If the box is in a high-traffic area, the cat may feel exposed and stressed.

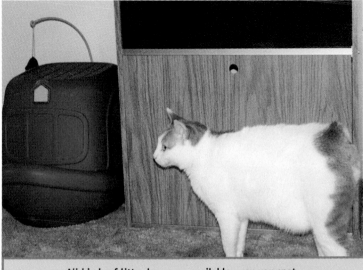

All kinds of litter boxes are available—can you spot the box in this picture? (It's hidden in the cabinet!)

for unwanted behavior related to the litter box. Consider what has recently changed in your home. Did you move the food and water so it is nearer to the litter? Move it back. Cats do not like the scent of a litter box near their food. Is the box in the way of a high traffic or play area? Again, it is probably easier to move the box than to move the traffic.

If these hints do not help, then consider the need to retrain the offender. To make using the box more attractive, try getting a bigger box, cleaning it more often, and filling it with different litter. You could also block off the box area completely. This move is particularly necessary when you need to treat the area to remove a scent and stain. If you cannot close the area off, try putting down a plastic carpet runner upside down with the small tips facing upward to discourage the cats from walking there.

Finally, litter box

problems may reflect overall problems in the home, and these may not just be problems with your cats. Stress in your home may incite stress in your cats. Your cats may be stressed if they are not getting enough exercise—if so, exercise them even more than you do now. Look to see if you have changed your schedule or your cat-care schedule. You may find, for example, that shifting the feeding times stresses a shy cat, and that stress is then causing the litter box problem.

EXCESSIVE SHYNESS AND SHUNNING

In the multiple-cat household, it is usually the aggressive cat, the active kitten, and the curious pair of friends that we notice. It takes a committed decision to watch out for the cat that is not seen so often, that is shy or hiding. This is not to say that shyness or hiding is

While most cats don't mind using a covered litter box, some cats don't like them. This could be because the box is not cleaned frequently or because the cat is shy and afraid of being surprised in the box.

A cat may become shy if she is continually harassed by other feline members of the household.

bad, but excessive shyness or hiding can be a problem or may be an indication that the cat is facing other problems.

Why is shyness a problem? An excessively shy cat may be reluctant to come out for feedings with other, more aggressive cats. Over a long period of time the shy cat may become undernourished or dehydrated as a result. Cats that are excessively shy may become problems because they are reluctant to come out to use litter boxes. They may break litter training because they flee from a litter box before they have completed elimination. Also, a cat that is very shy or that hides from

other cats is very difficult to deal with when she needs help because she is used to hiding. If you need to take her for inoculations, you may find it very difficult to catch her or even to find her.

What kinds of problems can excessive shyness indicate? First and foremost, a cat that seems to be very shy may in fact be shunned by the other cats. Many times, cats will shun another cat because that cat is ill. So, shunning may be an early warning of health problems.

Shunning also commonly occurs when a cat comes back from the veterinarian. The cats that did not go to the

doctor see an old friend returning, but they smell something else. That scent may just be of new people, but it could be the scent of other animals that the cats do not recognize. If a cat has had an operation, the smell of a veterinarian's office, particularly smells associated with surgery, could trigger an unpleasant reaction. The result is that the cats staying at home may temporarily shun a cat returning from a trip to the veterinarian. One way to avoid this is to use the same scent trick you used to introduce a new cat or kitten: Before releasing your cat from her carrier, put a little of one of your scents on her and on the cats greeting her as well. This measure will not remove

Shy cats are frequently a problem in the multiple-cat household. With so many other cats clamoring for attention, it can be hard to watch out for the cat that is less visible, but it is very important to monitor the shy cat's health and well being.

the "vet smell," but it will help assure the cats that the returning cat is one of them.

Excessive shyness may also indicate that your cat, if she comes from a background with which you are unfamiliar, may have been subjected to some trauma, such as abuse. While you cannot undo the past abuse, you can try to make sure that such a cat is very secure. Watch for signs that the cat is not actually shy, but is rather afraid of something that is not causing fear in the other cats. The fearful cat may be reacting to an object, a scent, or even a person's way of moving his hands. Once you have identified what triggers the fear, try to remove the cause from the environment. By doing that, you can make the shy cat less shy and more secure.

On a less serious note, if a cat is happy and content in your home, her shyness may indicate that she needs more socialization. Socialization is a slow process, requiring that you work with the cat daily, playing with her and providing her with security, reassurance, and a calm environment. The goal is to get the cat to resocialize with you and with other cats. Let her learn that she can depend on you and that she does not have to fear you.

Socializing a shy cat is a slow process, requiring that you work with the cat daily, playing with her and providing her with security.

RECORDS

Keeping records on your cats and kittens is a critical responsibility for the owner of a multiple-cat household. While you know what the special needs are of each of your cats—that is, which cat needs which food, which medication, or which type of special handling, if you do not have good records, *you cannot rely on anyone else* to have them either. To be realistic, there may come a day when someone else may need that record information.

For example, does your cat-sitter know how old each cat is? Do your neighbors know who your veterinarian is if there is a problem and you are not at home to deal with it? Do your family members and friends know how to care for your cats if you are sick—or worse?

What to Record

For each of your cats, you should keep a permanent record with *all* of the information that someone else who might have to come into your home would need in order to care for your cats and kittens as well as you do.

First, each cat should be described in ways that a person relatively unfamiliar with cats can understand. For example, don't say that a particular cat has a "beauty mark." Say the cat has a black spot on her left cheek. Also, make sure that the description helps a stranger understand which cat is which. So, if you have three red tabby cats, and they all look very much alike, find something that you can *easily* ascertain to tell them apart. For example, one of the three is probably the heaviest. In addition, take a picture of each cat, separately if you can, and mark it with the cat's name. If you have determined the weights of the cats, add that to the information, but note the date on which you weighed that cat.

All of the records should be indexed by the cat's name. If your cat has been known by several names, because you changed names over time, put down all of them. Why? Your veterinarian's office may have

You know the special needs of each of your cats, but it is important to keep a record of all the information in case you are unable to care for them.

If you have two cats that look alike, make sure to describe them carefully in your records. Label a picture of each cat with his or her name if necessary.

some of the medical records for that cat under two different names, when the records should be under one name.

After having described each cat, you should keep at least the following information current:

• Gender, as well as reproductive status, (that is, whole, spayed, or neutered) should be indicated. While all of your cats should be spayed or neutered, a new arrival might not have had the procedure yet. Also, keep copies of the spay and neuter certificates here.

• Note the locale your cat frequents. Is that cat limited to a particular room in the house? Does she try to sneak outside, so that you have to guard the back door?

• If you do not know the cat's birthdate, estimate the age with the help of your veterinarian. Then choose an approximate date of birth. It makes a lot more sense to say a cat was born "in 1997" than to say she is "three years old."

As of when was she three?

• Does this cat have to be fed special food? Does she need other special care, such as a daily ear cleaning?

• For each cat, you should indicate the date she received her most recent rabies shot. Keep the veterinarian's rabies vaccination certificate along with records of any other shots. Make sure your list

and your veterinarian's list are the same, particularly if you administer some of these shots yourself.

• Note special behavior. Does this cat play only with certain other cats? Is she afraid of a particular cat? If she hides from strangers, where does she usually go?

• Note medical history. What injuries has the cat suffered? Has she been diagnosed with any disease or other medical condition? Does the cat have to take regular medication or treatments? If so, what?

• Indicate the name, address, and telephone number of your veterinarian.

• If any of your cats are registered, pedigreed cats, you should keep copies of all registry paperwork in the file and also make sure that your records show that the cat you call Fluffy is actually registered under a fancy show cat name.

Where to Keep Records

Your information and lists should be kept where a third party, possibly a stranger, can find them. A good place would

On your records, note the locale your cat frequents. Can she usually be found with another cat? If so, which one?

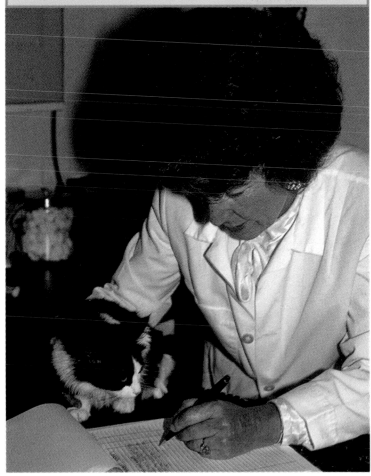

Your cat's pedigree, if she is a registered purebred, is just one example of the kind of records you should keep.

cats when you are away.

If you have a neighborhood watch or police drive-by service, the personnel probably will not want to keep these records, but inform them that you have such records and where they are. Hopefully they will never need to use them, but it would be good for them to know where they are if an emergency ever arose.

LOSSES AND EMERGENCIES

Whether you assume responsibility for the care of one cat or more cats, you should try to plan ahead for future unpleasantness while you are

be near your telephone or by your bed. But wherever you keep them, make sure that your veterinarian, your cat-sitter, and even your neighbors and family know that you have such records and where they are kept.

Who Should Get Copies of Records

After you have assembled your records, you should take a few moments and cross-check them with your veterinarian. For example, are your cats indexed at the veterinarian's office under the same names you use? Does the office record have an estimated date of birth, as does yours? To maintain complete records, you and your veterinarian may find that it is best for you to give a copy of your records to the office to keep for its own use.

Also, give at least a summary of your records to anyone who cares for your cats or who has a key to your house. Advise them that the records are updated, so that they should check your records if they have to care for your

Cross-check your records with those of your veterinarian. You may wish to give a copy of your records to the veterinarian to keep in her office.

Give a summary of your records to anyone who cares for your cats or has a key to your house. Let them know where you keep the full set of records.

Your cats will notice and react when another cat dies. They may seem to mourn—eating less, playing less, and generally being less animated.

enjoying the happiness your cats are bringing you now. Some unpleasant events are inevitable; others may never occur, although bad things *have* happened to other cat owners. You should plan for all of them.

Dealing with Loss for the Owner

Losing a cat is inevitable. Just like us, cats are living creatures, subject to accidents, illness, and eventually aging. If you have a cat that is ill, try not to treat her as if she were already dead, that is, by ignoring her or not calling her by name. Rather, try to share what time you still have.

When your cat companion dies, you will grieve. That is normal and natural. Do not suppress it. Let it happen, but do not let grief change your decisions. One of the biggest mistakes cat owners sometimes make is to go out and get another cat to "replace" a cat that has just died. Emotionally, that does not work. It often is merely an expression of our

When your cat dies, it is normal and natural to grieve. Do not suppress your emotions, but do remember that they will heal with time.

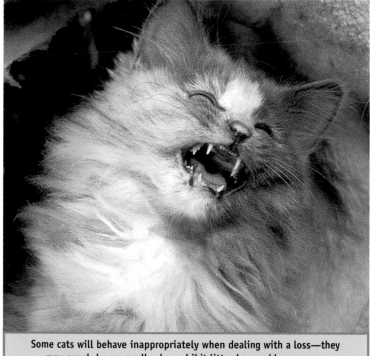

Some cats will behave inappropriately when dealing with a loss—they may growl, be unusually shy, exhibit litter box problems, or cry excessively. These behaviors will pass with time.

need to try to get past the pain of loss. However, adding to your feline family for this reason alone is not wise.

Instead, wait for the pain of the loss to pass. It will. While you are trying to recover from the loss, do not separate yourself from the rest of the cats. One of the most wonderful things that cats bring to their relationship with humans is the ability to calm us, to take our minds off of ourselves and our problems. Let your cats do that for you.

Dealing with the Cats' Reaction to the Loss of Another Cat

Many people do not realize that cats will notice the loss of another cat and will react to that. They do not react as humans do—for they are not humans. Rather, they react in their own way and recover in their own time.

The most common situation where we see this reaction is when a few cats have spent many years together, and then one dies. Sometimes one or more of the others appear to mourn: They eat less, play less, and are less animated. In part, this is because they do not have the stimulation of a longtime friend's company. They will gradually come out of this. Many people think that the answer is a new cat—often a new kitten. Actually, this will not often work, and may even backfire. That is because you are now trying to introduce a strange, active creature to a cat that is older, set in her ways, and less active then she was formerly.

Other cats dealing with a loss may behave inappropriately: They may growl at cats they used to

cuddle with, be unusually aggressive or shy, or stop using the litter box. The solution is to help these cats by removing the objects or cats to which they are reacting. Change the environment if they seem to be aggressive toward a certain object. Replace familiar litter boxes with newer (or older) ones. Temporarily separate the cats until everyone is more settled.

What we often do not appreciate is that these cats are not only dealing with the change in their own environment, they are often reacting to *our* grief and pain. As we heal, they will tend to return to normal.

Caring for Your Cats After You Are Gone

None of us are comfortable discussing our own mortality, but we have to face that inevitability. Remember, your cats, living indoors with good veterinary care, now have a life span of 15 or even 20 (or more) years. So as you age, they will be growing older (and better) with you.

Consider who can care for your cats if you are hospitalized for a long time or die. Is anyone willing to provide cat care? Have you asked anyone? Have you told them where all of your records are?

While you can leave money in your will to people, you cannot leave money directly to your cats, no matter what you hear, so do not try this. Talk to your attorney about this issue. Usually the best you can do is to arrange for someone to care for your cats, and leave them some money to help them pay for the care the cats require.

If this is not an option, look into facilities such as life-care, no-kill shelters where your cats can be cared for permanently. There are very few such facilities, and you must make arrangements for such care well in advance. The type of arrangements you will have to make differs in each case. Whatever you do, plan and arrange for something. Remember, if you do not make arrangements for the care of your cats, no one else will.

Evacuations and Emergency Planning

You have already spent a lot of time and money making your home comfortable and safe for your cats. Now you must also plan for the possibility that you may have to care for your cats in adverse circumstances, or that you and your cats may have to leave your home quickly.

What do we mean by adverse circumstances? If you live in the Northeast or Midwest US, you should be planning for the fact that you could face a major blizzard any winter. In the central US, in parts of the South and West, local floods, while not threatening a home, may cut you off from stores and your veterinarian for days at a time, even if evacuation is unnecessary. The same is true for forest and brush fires in many areas, as well as localized problems ranging from a loss of electric power to

While you can leave money in your will to people, you cannot leave money directly to your cats, no matter what you may have heard.

You may have to care for your cats under adverse circumstances, or you may have to leave home quickly in an emergency. This doesn't mean that your cats have to sleep in a suitcase, but you should be prepared.

Suppose there is a major blizzard and you are unable to get to the store—do you have enough supplies on hand for yourself and your cats?

chemical spills.

So what can you do? You should plan for two alternatives:

• Isolation. For example, you are unable to leave your home and get to stores for food or litter or to your veterinarian or pharmacist for treatment or medical supplies. Also, you should consider if you are vulnerable to a loss of power or water.

• Evacuation. You and your cats are forced to leave your home, probably with little or no warning.

For isolation, make sure that you have on hand at least one week's worth of cat food *and* litter. In some areas, you should have two weeks' worth. Also, do you have water in case the power is out (which for some of us cuts off water)? What about the medicines your cats (and you) need? Do you have enough to last you long enough?

To make sure that you do not dig into this emergency stock, one trick is to keep it separate from all of your other supplies. That way, you avoid the temptation to dip into these supplies. We call this emergency stock our "winter shelf." In the spring, when the threat of being snowed in has vanished, we bring most of this stock back into use. Still, we always keep some reserves on hand.

Evacuation is another matter entirely. If you and your cats have to evacuate, you will typically have very little notice. The reasons for evacuation are more numerous than most of us want to think about. They include fire (at your home or next door), flood, storm damage to your roof, a chemical spill or explosion on a nearby road, a police emergency nearby, etc.

There are two kinds of evacuations—those where you have a warning, such as news that a river is rising, and those for which there is no warning, such as the arrival at your door of a fireman due to a chemical spill down the street.

When you have a warning, you have time to plan where you will be going and to find and collect every one of your cats. If there is no warning, you had better be prepared to act.

How well will you and your cats handle a terrifying emergency? Prevent panic with good planning.

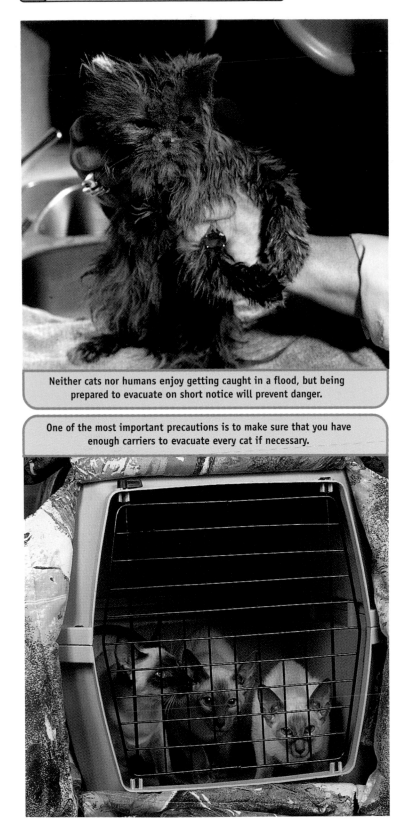

Neither cats nor humans enjoy getting caught in a flood, but being prepared to evacuate on short notice will prevent danger.

One of the most important precautions is to make sure that you have enough carriers to evacuate every cat if necessary.

First, you should assemble an emergency kit if you are in an area where evacuations are often threatened, or where you may have to evacuate without any help. Include in the kit a credit card, cash, a cell phone if possible, your medications, your cats' medications, your veterinarian's name and telephone number, and your personal telephone book. If you can, take some food. Do not worry about litter—you can always use newspapers if you have to.

When there is no warning, you must already be prepared. That means that before an emergency occurs, make sure you have enough carriers to evacuate every cat. If you do not have enough carriers, get them. In the meantime, if necessary, you can use a trick developed by emergency services workers: In an emergency evacuation, cats can be placed in strong, large pillowcases that are then tied shut. There is plenty of air for the cats, so they can be carried out of a house in this manner. Remember, when you open the pillowcase, you will have one very mad cat. Once you have enough carriers, place them around your house so that you will have a carrier near at hand wherever you have cats.

Once you are out of the house, think carefully. Where will you be going? If you have to stay away for a long while, can you take care of cats where you are going, or should you choose another place? Planning for emergencies is very hard because, by their very nature, emergencies tend to defeat planning. At least you will be able to get yourself and all of your cats away from a threat if you have done some planning.

The multiple-cat household has special care requirements. From time to time, you may need help in providing that care. There are also times when you must plan for the care of your cats when you are away overnight or longer.

TO BOARD OR NOT TO BOARD

In general, the best thing you can do for your cats is to provide care for them in your home, rather than have the cats go out for boarding. This is for the following reasons:

• Your cats are familiar with their surroundings. They are comfortable and secure there. They have worked out among themselves which cats go where and when they go.

• Boarding facilities vary widely in the accommodations they offer. Some keep each cat separate, and others keep them in groups. If cats can be boarded together, you must determine which cats can accompany which others and which cats must be separated. That may not be easy to do.

• It is almost always more costly to board cats than it is to have a caregiver come in.

• The travel to and from a boarding facility may cause stress or even distress for some of your cats.

This is not to say that you should never considering boarding one or more cats. Boarding can be very important if, for example, you have one or more cats that need special medical attention, such as shots or pills at regular intervals. The boarding facility staff routinely provides such care.

WHEN DO YOU NEED HELP?

Anytime you expect to be away from home overnight, you should always make sure that someone at least stops by. When they do, they should, at a minimum, check on all of your cats, freshen the water and food, and scoop waste from every litter box. While cats can adjust to you being out of the house emotionally, they have physical needs that must be tended to every day. Number one among these needs is the continuous availability of fresh water.

By having someone stop by to do these basic chores, you are also making sure that there are no problems that could cause difficulties for your cats. For example, if the power went off for a time while you were away in the summer, the caregiver could go around to partially open windows or adjust the thermostat to help reduce the

For most cats, accompanying you while you travel is not their idea of fun. A good cat-sitter can provide peace of mind for you and your pets.

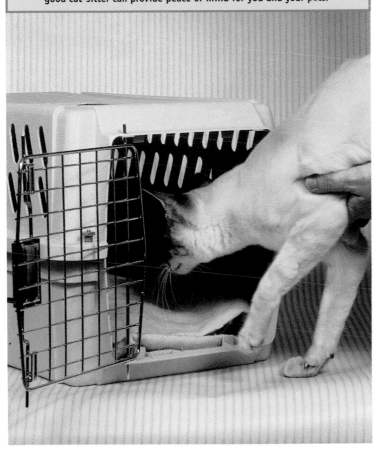

Most cats dislike being boarded at a kennel or veterinary clinic. If at all possible, you should arrange for your cats to be cared for in your home when you are away.

"How long will my owner be gone?"
Most cats can cope with your absence just fine for a few days,
but they still need basic daily care.

temperature buildup caused by the temporary lack of air conditioning.

If you are ill or injured, the work involved in caring for your cats will not stop. Rather than try to reduce what you do, such as scooping but not cleaning cat boxes as regularly, try to get someone in to help you. This will keep your multiple-cat household cleaner, your home more comfortable for your recuperation, and your cats happier and healthier. Even if you feel well enough to handle the food, water, and litter, remember those of your cats that have special needs. For example, if you sprain your ankle, and for a week can walk only with a cane, just how will you be able to catch Fluffy, the cat that needs to take a pill every day? You can't. In addition, by getting help, you will speed your own recovery.

Finally, you may want some help just to give yourself some time off. For example, suppose you are planning to go out for your birthday, and your friends have planned a full day for you—lunch, shopping, sightseeing, late dinner. Wouldn't it be nice to come home and find that the basic chores had all been completed? Time off from chores can be a welcome physical and mental respite.

DEALING WITH CAT-SITTERS

Increasingly, cat owners are turning to cat-sitters to provide care for their cats when they are not home. Pet-sitting has become a major business in some parts of the country. If you are considering using a cat-sitter, there are several things you should do before you just open the yellow pages and telephone one to come in and care for your cats over a long weekend:

• Ask your veterinarian for suggestions on possible sitters. In addition to sitters who provide care as a business, your veterinarian may know of competent individuals who have let him or her know that they would like to do some cat-sitting. This might even include a member of the office staff.

• Interview the cat-sitter, that is, the individual who would be coming in, before you decide to use the service. Some sitter services have a number of employees. While it is good to meet the owner, you must meet the sitter. Do it at your home so you can see how the cats and the sitter react to each other there.

• Ask the service for references, particularly from other multiple-cat owners. Then call them and ask how they rate the service when compared with others. You may find that they use two services. If so, ask for a contact at the other one. Also, ask if they used other services and stopped, and why they chose to discontinue the service. You may be able to avoid an unhappy experience.

• Discuss pricing and services up front to avoid surprises. Many cat-sitter services charge per cat. In the multiple-cat household, you should negotiate a fee based more on actual time spent providing care. Why? First, the time spent driving to the house is the same whether you have one cat or six cats. Also, you probably do not have one litter box per cat; there are probably fewer boxes than there are cats. In the multiple-cat household, the cats are usually fed in groups. That means that one canned food feeding or one dry chow dispenser refill may serve several cats. The upshot is that caring for six cats is usually not six times as much work as caring for one cat.

• Find out about availability and flexibility. Can you book the service in advance? Can you rely on getting a sitter on short notice? If you cannot get home on time due to travel problems, will the service continue to come in to care for your cats until you come home? If the sitter serving you gets sick, is there a backup?

• Is the service bonded? Remember, you will be giving the service a key to your home.

WHAT TO TELL CAREGIVERS

First, tell the caregiver where you are going, where and when you can be reached, and when you will be back. The best way to do this is to leave a written message. When you return, call the caregiver after you have checked to make sure everything is all right.

Second, tell your caregiver the name, address, and telephone number of your veterinarian. Make sure the caregiver knows how to get there. Tell the caregiver that in case of emergency, he or she is to call your own veterinarian first. Some cat-sitters have a backup veterinarian they use if you do not make special arrangements. You may also have to leave your veterinarian a signed consent to treat your cats in your absence in cases of emergency.

Third, make sure that the caregiver (and any potential substitutes) know where you keep your cat records. Then tell them not only where you keep your regular supplies, but also your emergency supplies, the backup food, and backup litter.

Fourth, show them where each of your evacuation cages or other evacuation supplies are located. Explain how to use them if there is an emergency.

Fifth, slowly walk your caregiver though the entire house. If possible, do this on a day before the caregiver is coming in to take care of your cats. Show the caregiver each cat, even if you have to bring out a shy cat to make the cat familiar with the caregiver and the caregiver familiar with the cat. Point out where the cats are fed, where the water is to go, which litter boxes should be cleaned, and which should be refilled with which particular litter products, if you use a variety

There are lots of times that you may require the services of a cat-sitter. For example, if you are ill or injured, someone else will have to care for your cats.

Increasingly, cat owners are turning to cat-sitters to provide care for their cats when they are not home. Pet-sitting has become a major business in some parts of the country.

of litters. If you have cats that need to be given any medication, have the caregiver show you how he or she intends to give the medication. A cat that you can easily give a pill may be difficult for the caregiver, or vice versa. If the caregiver is not comfortable giving medications, you may want to consider boarding that particular cat, possibly with your veterinarian.

Sixth, explain to the caregiver how the household cat hierarchy works. Which cats are the dominant ones? Which cats do not like to be with each other? Where are the best hiding places? What areas of the house are off-limits to particular cats and why?

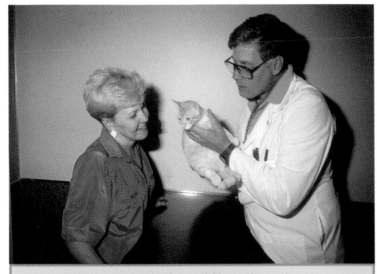

When you are looking for a reliable cat-sitter, ask your veterinarian for recommendations.

Many cat-sitting services charge by the cat, but the multiple-cat owner may wish to negotiate a fee based on actual time spent providing care.

Explain to your cat-sitter how the household cat hierarchy works. Introduce her to every cat and show her all of their hiding places. That way, she can "take inventory" each time she visits.

Tell others who your caregiver is and how to reach the caregiver. Your veterinarian should know who your sitter is, and so should a friendly neighbor. In some parts of the nation, the police maintain profiles on homes that are on a special watch while the owners are away traveling or on vacation. Tell the police not only that you are away each time that you leave, but also that your cat-sitter will be coming in. Otherwise, the police may stop your cat-sitter. Give them the sitter's name and telephone number as well. If there is an emergency while you are away, your sitter will be close enough to enable the police to get in or to get your cats to the veterinarian before you could ever hope to get home.

Make sure your pet-sitter has the name, address, and telephone number of your veterinarian in case of emergency. Your veterinarian may also require your signed consent to treat your cats in your absence.

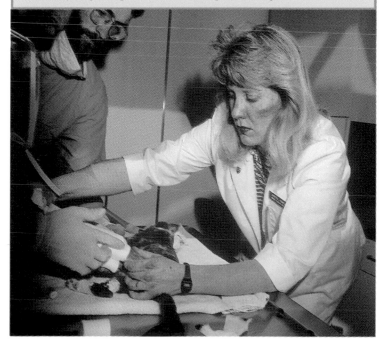

Suggested Reading

WW 074
Myth & Magic of Cats
Arianna Reynolds
64 pages, more than 75 full-color photos

WW 041
Choosing the Perfect Cat
Dennis and Eve Kelsey-Wood
64 pages, more than 75 full-color photos

TS 302
Cat Health Encyclopedia
Edited by Dr. Lowell Ackerman
320 pages, more than 200 full-color photos

TS 253
Cat Behavior and Training
Dr. Lowell Ackerman
320 pages, more than 200 full-color photos

TS 251
Owner's Guide to Cat Health
Dr. Lowell Ackerman
208 pages, more than 100 full-color photos

TS 250
Skin and Coat Care for Your Cat
Dr. Lowell Ackerman
160 pages, more than 100 full-color photos